hotel universo

hotel universo

Chris Brown

PUNCHER & WATTMANN

First published in 2021
Published by Puncher and Wattmann
PO Box 279
Waratah NSW 2298

http://www.puncherandwattmann.com
puncherandwattmann@bigpond.com

NATIONAL
LIBRARY
OF AUSTRALIA

A catalogue entry for this book is available from the National Library of Australia.

ISBN   9781925780796

Cover design by Miranda Douglas
Typesetting by Morgan Arnett
Printed by Lightning Source International

Contents

A balancing act

or delicate shot

out of the dunes

leaves you
just ten seconds

to enter the frame.

-

More than our share of sun-worship out here

shining the badge to esteem in a sequence mapping East –
a glass box

bolted to a cliff

chalking pastel fibro

decluttered

gone
if not for long

then moving house

and leaving priceless art on the confused
space of a footpath

-

I own I grew up here

own

I live in the sprawl

same pledge to postcode
inked in on the knuckles

art that's mainly tracings

-

In the park

flipping through fotos
you can't find so words

will do?

same page I wonder where had I been days
ago the first time as it will be different next

-

-

A boat of great size draws up to the window.
South of Commandant Morriset's private pool
reconstructed sandscapes and access closures.
Shhhhhhh SHHHHHhhhhh: surf at your door.
I can hear it from here though mainly at night
when the tucked-in traffic rests no sooner

rubble in the garden where the river ends.
The new house on the beach at Dixon Park
like a scale model of the National Library
but more glass.

at new year

white, volcanic

   cloudbank a broken wave

on the low horizon

summer suddenly

   short of breath, a sunset

illuminates clouds of dust

where kids make goal-posts

   of two towering scribbly gum.

slide lower lock the windows

are they syntax

   and later

like the light

I weaken,

   dreaming up a promise

occasion alone calls *resolution*

clamour at daybreak

snake (slough) cicada shell self re-invent

and move on…edging the old coal route

every hopeful sapling framed

shadow spilt down all three lanes

in this heavy weather

lawns are islands

blue humidity seated

in a blend of couch/buffalo

surrey the garden of england

ours the beer-garden

wind gusts to animate

a lone wooden lorikeet

paddling this way, that

simultaneously,

corrugated plastic

throws warped shadow. rain weighed

in the skin of a shade-sail

patterns of unpredictability

our relief - brief exit

driving now

a low-rise window

frames *the flag.*

(are we just Misguided Love?)

hung on a garden's

post-storm stillness.

resin scent of eucalyptus.

Home, I haven't heard

a word

of *What I'm Listening To.*

village pieces

Some rabble moved in next door meaning us

wave anyway this side of the leafy path and

    light industry

rob frost fencing his differences i pass as you

climb ramps and losing the radio vanish in a

monolith's aisles of bright nebula hangars of

    paint and pine

Imperatives of the leisure precinct enervate

    though home

    pleads ignorance

you peek through blinds like a fallen mirror

I'm on the backseat thinking things through

the underwater window of another's lenses

not staring at soliloquies peopling bus-stops

    we'll wait on

japanese friends and foreign english cinema

call a guest the better guide chat roleplay in

textbook coffee shops portmanteau hybrids

looping forelegs of chairs and aren't we all

real bodies at rogue intersections just chance

meetings bright faces eclipsing bigger plans

boats and trams

riding on the wrong

side of the road might

be hard to get used to

like phrasebook philosophy

or vertical stairs'll

get us nowhere

but fishing in the cbd

surfing in the river

whatever the season

dense low-level cloud

chokes the coffee shop

too busy figuring the ring

road an umbrella for two

cite same chain store on the

corner by the bridge similitude

at the tired *thus* emotional end

of town (the map lost) at last

a place to park the bike a fire

nightfall fell unnoticed

in those chapters

northern line (the blue one)

false start then shut the gate.
as fig roots ripple & fissure
the asphalt up ahead an earth

mover rattles its chain of prints
down the clay artery a tallish figure
waistcoat to match his rubber cones

bends steeply grinding the uneven
joins in the concrete. a bell chimes
once around the square. each day

its own; lived here too long - stop to
ask someone a tourist what a street
sign means to 'small town' semiotics.

a gentle somewhat deceptive incline
(not a hill) & like last night line-endings
override a silence to amplify the in-breath

that's the heart speaking. woken
to you or out late walking home
ears still ringing a front porch night

light automates. bad dreams
where the body rules. shelter
in your own evasive shadow.

& the escalators are resting as stairs.
some tremor there as in a deep impression.
penury's cup half empty.

divine ascent select exit the footpath

steps off in sudden relief where the leaves
find the gutters & you still can't remember

a thing you were thinking.

New body/legs

A new regime and daily now we count each step.

We find there's life and body yet in the vicarious

data. Or a pulse. That compensates sleep as each

new day's industry diligence attentions to detail.

Wipe sleep from your eyes and mysteries remain –

red leaves or faded rainbows an old finance rag

weather-proofed and footing the rivering drive.

Coasting by you lugged the water on your back.

And by this we've forgotten ourselves let go our

destination (pain). Then I urge you keep talking

to me. Put the cruel personified hills behind us.

books and records (and Chekhov)

wake up and smell the
milk and black coffee
sleep in and go out at
09:26 and 28 degrees
but seconds ago
cooks hill books every
room in the house its own
genre half *fiction* skimread
and a stylus skating dust
in the audible distance
know the song not the title
nor the   words   not much
more than the melody really
on tiptoes handpick the lady
and the little dog and other stories
alternate title: try future cruelties –
tonight ol' Petrov'll tell the beggars of Ukleyevo:
god'll feed yer – but that's Petrov

The nocturnal ceremonies

There are the turnstiles to NUMBER EIGHT
or the dealer's codes compulsion ignores.

Your basement: globe blown...drowsy end
ings unresolved if morning brings me up to date.

I lie at the faint-of-breath
curtains of a bay window

painted shut   ...sky's
curfew   sky clears.

When you put
the tv on and

Guilt me in the guest-room (from which
all sound carries) I'll have my humanity to blame.

The fugitive scales the fence skims the bonnet
and backtracks as any roving beam of blue moonlight testifies.

Broad daylight

Private screenings of a propertied subjective ex
cess a raking breeze a blade of grass in it issues
with line is there a latitude for those coordinates?

Mid-morning bareness if that's possible the sort
of absence we've defrayed in xerophytes i watch
star trak and toll down the street thought they
were coming here

We're on the verandah reading poems –
concrete forms as duly redirect the eye

There's a smashing image of an incandescent
interior out by the road evicted mirrors host
double roses

We sit in (above) traffic await a passing train
whatever it erases and restores a triple mast
or strip of sky a bridge the sun

burns down right down to about
eye level down and
and on

Awe-stralian sublime

Cool and warmer air sparring in a doorway.
An island locked in the arms of its interior.
Here a photo of a dust-storm in the rough
shape of Uluru on a shelf in the post office
(Also a bottlo and a papershop). If that's not
country enough the new year streets are quiet
seeming wider ("town's dead" said the driver).
And the weather's reel of matching icons till
Salvation. Still games will be fixtures so look
alive! Their shirts: bold and self-referencing.
You can watch the game as you play it...back.
Trees and machines make up the ambience.
You don't miss what isn't there until it's ___.
(Instant still rings louder than a latent hum.)
We can't pick smoke not even wind-affected
vestigial flight from cloud. Plan becomes
confusion. Ash monument. "It happened
so quickly."

Scenic

the scenic assembling
the stage properties of daily life
to press a tableau a
take on the field
east of Strzelecki

white sea-mist and
censure in the skies
our conversation
cut by war games
out of Williamtown

they're flying too close
to the high seas
and cliffs
to disregard resumes
marked departures

the pleasure
of the performance
of the drive: flash chrome
grill nudging the
glass

vexed monorhyme
or lyric's hard luck
that won't wash
at those set
edges

neighbour
conscientious
where nurture's a method

so diffuse I pass in a
veiling mist

but then if you insist
how leave you out?
scenic: assembling
adapted for the
page stage
page stage
page

hotel universo

bowties or butterflies –
the sauce of your choice.

an umbrella collapses.
the chairs inseparable.

\-

this display a glass
bottomed gondola.

model train derailment
halfway up a mountain

\-

then restless in the
method of immersion

la lingua madre
surfaces for breath.

\-

pine needles carpet
the terra rossa tennis court.

imminent arrival –
text-to-destination.

\-

digging deep for lost vocab

souvenirs

his own little
piece of vesuvius.

-

...*cinema centrale*
mapping out

the monolingual
provinces

-

not corrupted
or embalmed

decomposition
of body and gown

-

coins rain
and thank

you gesture
the eyes of the mime

-

the radio
guide's tale

of the twins

history and hearsay

-

and out of a tower's
skinny staircase

the renaissance
spills into the backyard

-

and all the
pillion riders

shirt-tails billow
on the past

village pieces iii

the leafy borough's

        leafage at the grate
        static on the waves

    hard sell   neuro

                    plastic
       ity

          via the capital

      head up −

for the lack

    a way in

    we'll take

    it! if a

       touring welsh chorus
       humours the guard

         among us −

          personifying

      take it!

          just now

the breadline
out the door

at Uprising

quiet   but answers at

our feet   where sparrows dare

                or walking
and some lyceen or local saint posts

a rainbow heart   at the
                red letterbox

                daily
we await its erasure...dissent and no
                one to de

        face it?

                yea or nay

        but auguring a
        c

b (collect
                ive

    best)

                this café

        replays of yesterday

out of the shadows

loyals
locals

take a chance

whisk their
crumbs and alms

                  to roost

an air letter

to Juanita,

Late fall if i can call it that

not that the weather cares

Know you're not at home?

at the streetcar stop wear the effects

of the bloor street snowplough

bow wave

Ottawa-coteau-?-montreal

in a bilingual province

i have half a language

less though the label

turned or page opposing

seemed somehow sympathetic

Emotional distance — is always

in miles and if the island prison

library's an escape

writing the air letter was

taking my homesickness pills

or you write *i* wait

though it's not us just the mail

the more prescient of beginnings

dear j, hope this finds you

City

Fritz Lang's

canted D(e)utch

(e) by day

by night

a name

on the sky.

Not quite

pyramids

but white coal

in conical

piles.

Meanwhile

behind

the trembling

shelves

groundlings

make up scale

wet down the open cut be

neath the crane

and chewed

union ensign

trailing.

Meanwhile

a mayoral ballot

in a prayer-hall

or impulse at

the top

or hope

in indecision.

"Conversation

meet dialogue."

The network's

a non-sequitur

the renaissance

just a waste

before the lither

lux rail slid

through.

"Tomorrow…"

though if this

is the future

why are

the signs

littering the

overpass stills?

Why won't

this clock

correct itself

like others?

Bikes and

trams among

the visions

we've enfutured.

Meanwhile

a guy in a red

cap and loud vest

herds his train

of lost trolleys

across the car

park. It's years

after workers

became Jobs.

It's open (never

closes). Nothing's

reclaimed.

Not a soul

leaves empty

handed.

Series

Tilt the screen
    from negative

so we can all see
    a next episode of the

poxy eviscerated
    middle ages

from the heights
    of millennial immunity

will

you.

What freedom
    to waste the hero

in the first act
    seasons to come

contriving others
    relieving

the early loss
    but making epic's

lord and lineage
    the closer

historical

example.

Well it isn't
the eldest boy

Will

dis

owns *his*
immodest

lot.

Ask anyone:
        a noble's
        pride's a public

bar. But why complain?
        What might

the people's princess
        say when so many

sit the best bit
        out looking pretty

and the part
        surveying the

slaughter from
        afar. *How* many

seasons

in a day?

Tempos

Filtered light half

a tablet half moon

the night of the fires

grey-out on Town

sun goes

benign to the eye

\-

Just a temperature

like go home

put your feet up

if that's what

you're doing

try again

this time with

less care

\-

Over conversation

some enchantment

or musical mystery

with detectives

who can sentence

conjecture

just like that

if you need to know

names

we cancel satellite

and keep the dish

-

Work ends days

become one

No I can't read speed

as it is written

yes I do

slow down for you

-

I have the tapes

but nowhere to play them

content to veto longing

no notes no ghosts no

histories in the digital

new critical just the

music

primo no

interruptions

solicitations

mood and decade

but I don't feel like

decade

or not that decade

just now

not right now

-

Though techno a

neighbour tells me's

for any hour

or voices in a yard

or hose on concrete

hose in bucket

passing bus

that cozy right on up

to our very devout

and yawningly longitudinal study

to language so patient

in your indecision

(track *those* changes)

and every day

has this wholesome

habit of reminding

some days go faster

than others and all

go faster than those

between

as you go

i.

Highways

scenic (past)/

present

ii.

Trade and

the ready tooth

of the caliph driving it

iii.

Sepsis sand snow

in empire's riding boots –

your tragedy our trivia

iv.

Express lanes

assumed democracies

roads to Wonder:

v.

(Effect

of novelty

upon ignorance.)

vi.

The eye-rolling street view and

white autonomous van

chalking data

vii.

for the

Your Place in Space

directory

viii.

Anywhere's a port

gate

hub

ix.

Each city's

unseen

periferi

x.

Swayed

by

transit

xi.

but brush a screen

the whole ground

shifts

Vis(i)tors

i.

office and library
cooling system hum
outside the weather

feet on pedal or dash
we refuel loyal listeners
tolerating radio's sight gags
took the bridge coming in

ii.

      here —
Port Botany sky
curators race for cover

our late 80s archive
an amateurish mix of creams and whites —
      is the view you paid for (sixteen replays
            are inconclusive)

iii.

a famous face *what'shisname*

     a red flag

the beach open
when it's closed…

iv.

    : almost on cue
a breeze reports
first in the crumbling architecture
        stippling windward

tracking the flown inflatable
        as far as

               White Cliffs

v.

when the kids get tired
the big kids get wired
when the kids get wired...

we have a boat out front
the adulation of the gulls
french for welcomes/
        farewells

vi.

time/location

peremptory bus doors

card in the lock

vii.

timed cued to cross

a short flight home
to spurred ledges

and where
walking ends
traipsing begins

i folly the signs

Ngarigo

i.

You set a dashboard in the foothills
everything traced located
and something like life's
entire transit history
brings you to this point
and coordinate otherwise irreducible

People used to summer here
when antique infinitives
were still a thing

You're pointing out
true conjectural North

talking
up Europe and
all the names we've been

We brush down
and pack out
Phytophthera in tow

Little prints and life-signs
box speakers in a casuarina
some sleepless reel
revising existential
hypotheses

Then an upward snowy drift
of ash and smoke

We're miles out

with nothing we can't
momently ascertain

draw down from stars
they hold all the
answers

ii.

Crimped heat over royalla estate
we lose you in it
waves and scraped hills
and homes unpacked
a w i d e land
this
to zoom out step
back won't do arrive
race down if nature
needs a witness

we swam in ice
and froze
and thawed
by fire
the sun came up
on people preparing
for popular extremes
when someone said you
you'll be right you can summit
          in a pram

the sky overhead
and your pathological camera
bird rock
winding creek
the best
and plainest
toponymies
if regal
names
do 0 for place

From this vantage
pointing out the
unseen
(N-facing)
snakes solar
butterflies and
wildflowers
scatter your
hiking
uniform

Signs for
or actual
Antipodean
elk
a bipolar
Winterhaus
heat in waves
on the double
illusion of Lake
George

By your credo

A skywritten holy
wish and you thought
a tag on a carriage an
optimal visibility some
gesture: for ephemera
it's grandiose

All topical I mean
obvious but irresistible
so leave it alone
crowds checking out and
these we relish to tell you are
just the minor triggers

Just an ad small fee
for what we receive
and that reminds me
mostly unopposed
to here this the present
though the endless odd-intentioned

prompts (LIVE DREAM (no pressure
no pressure)) seem helpful
in their way…dials climb
may rave yet tangentiality
was never madness here

No risk like impunity –
so do it…borderline at
the wheel coasting quietly
home and dismissing the real
the lights and omens those tedious
but mainly spectral police on the trail

Maps of my transitory past

(May in Melbourne)

I hand the blue pleated curtain to the fleeting
Feeling a bit abused the way the cabin looked
After fifteen hours but leaving nothing behind.
Open spaces then the grid and tilt to shelves of
Vacant strata (loading...) some exposed scopic
Ledge at a misty lean. This precinct has sharp
Teeth but not for pedestrians less *Les Pietons*
De Mai! Fresh even now. Skaters' idle grace
In the park of countermeasures and collared
Elms and stairs stacking up to soft concrete
Landings. Only so much order. Not a regular
Knave among the artists merchants purvey
Ors. But ask any blind cop: in a matraquage
There's nought to see and we'd better run. A
Long. Days of rain. The gutters refuse the
stars and stare out to sea. We offer feed
back we mend the greener strips of the
Broken cycleway breach twin rail to the
Gendered dorm of a converted nunnery.
It isn't half the exile it used to be. Cosmo
Polites keep the oddest hours communal
Bookcases the best of hugo for a rainy day.
Cities patch our coats cry *proust* for cheers.
It pays to update the folks to pin these and
Other relics to your graphic trail the weight
Less map of your immediate transitory past.

Echo on Vico Solitaria

This hill town's stairwells
softened by linen sunning on the lanes.
Streets too tight for cars: but tributaries
down to publicca or plebiscito. A porch
and double door watched by lions
legs crossed.

When life resumes round four
word on the street's a song
I like whose lyric eludes me
though cobbled Vico Solitaria
echoes as if to compensate.

Tonight I've turned off
messenger and make my lists.
Tomorrow's museum models
an incomplete past: the sweet
torsos of acephalous empire.

Don't go looking for the English channels

Listen for years
before you speak

but that's not
what they say

this the best program
outside shops/streets

He'd liked to see
that film again

with subtitles
the one about

the holy roman
mouth

after me —
erre (si) *erre*

He'd waited so long
returning customer

his tongue precedes
him as a sort of

recourse to gesture
so met in his own

whole
tenses

missing
later chapters

still brand
new

He types the code
that gives him access

to the flat
puts the tv on

there's always local
backed by satellite

in ubiquitous

L'il England

Port

Clipped pines
       at the bow
of the New Expedition.

Cormorant Rd.
       Kooragang
and its windows tight.

A most extant
       most human
       geography. *Post*

       present as
premature

memory. Are we
late

yet?

-

We leave it
walk this hill

that goes up
to give us
depth
as colour
and that other

warp across the peak
to map and metaphor.

Clipped pines
at the bow
of the Honest Sky.

If *the sea-harbour is*
        in me tell me
I am not in the harbour.

The Honest Sky is (in
the harbour) land light

in the iron hold of the

        Honest

Sky.

Daylong

Some arrant will

and a kettle catching

damp in the fireplace.

Warm rhythm

and winter fleece

that feels so good

I call the office

reach the machine

I'm quietly hoping for.

(Moods for space

and their vague apologies.)

Tea and toast.

This window's dove

or mushroom visibility.

Roads blacker with rain.

For a while

then cold abeyance

object in the absence

of its given-ness. I re

heat the tea dis

card the milk skin

watch sport's replays

forays about

a walled defence

feint turning inches into acres

of cantering

daylight.

-

-

Saturday

a deep blue sky

when the sun sets

rock-like Faith

in the figures

out of Penrith

our feelings

in a scatter plot

or line-graph.

Business-

as-

usual

as usual

and never yet

inured

Liege

A lighter mood then drawn like gravity

and ground given

because He has that kind of magnetism

my loveless heart

less crush.

When the lights go down

gloom as genre:

who needs a syllabus?

Early myths we read

made real

now that you own

the weather.

Kids take up

online battles

and can't sleep.

They worry at

old young white men.

Let's make all our mighty toads and lords

petty trolls

to blink away

not tease

with "no reply".

Okay?

Promise?

It's how we

say goodnight.

That new secretary in the House:

     light-footed liege to the abject

     their star ascending. We get

active in North Lambton.

Unheard/seen if we speak

in poems.

Light beer

Kneeling seemed perfect for an anthem?

For such occasions

we pour light beer only —

"Piss-weak"

red on blue

on green

Mere stripling once —

look at him now

("finds a man in space")

Light beer

shit call:

replay

selective

replay

Grit by sea

Histories cut by hand
and the back as proof.
Attrition: anchored
in rocks and violacea.

Mythic head of kelp.
Release through a lull.
Waves with no place
else to break trace the
reef beneath a sea spray

rainbow and spidery
drone eyeing hot new
talent a few faded stars.
The shit pipe's a pier

by mid-tide! and a
pilot can't be found.
You get dolphins for
your birthday and
a polished stone...

Gifts for gulls. Take some
cuttlefish for the finches.
Tidal e/co/tox/ico/log/ical
process at our feet.

signs say

the new year
      sorting the nonnecessary
            so much to go through

            the end of an era
      kids start school

      if hours race by
            without word
others are less
            forthcoming

            and what
impasse looks like
            we leave it

      all behind
            push out in our fresh airs
                  and don't even

            wait for a sign

if the subway
      gets a lick of paint to patch over's
            to apply a ground

            and everything

            "in walking distance"

            ....walking distance

of the lawns of Pius knee-high
                    for the summer break

walking distance of the way the image disseminates
                    and
knows no limit
                    and wins its salience

like luminous bodies
          visibilities we can abide

                    or accommodate
          when so little
                              else is on hold

through/by(e)

After Pelican the Black Swan Hotel
                                        (Swansea)
then the F1 and a "last chance for fuel"

Pseudo Echo are playing the Doyalson
the 19th and hey that's today tonight!

though we're just passing through —

MANGOS CHERRIES NECTARINES

                                        (acrylic

                                        on ply)

"Sydney's. Best. Rock"   's an oyster

The Hawkesbury tells you   roads
                                     aren't rivers...

a streaming prefab frieze   still
                                     we're active
passengers   and the radio

Student rapport

The teacher is upset because he can
hardly hear himself in the democracy.

In another paradigm the bells are still ringing we steal
in from truancy's private beach

over nightingale floors. Father has
an aneurism but mum's okay with it...

crises of distrust
acquittal's embroidered diaries

-

Jacob called Jackson *weird*
which wasn't so strange –
from one as *conforming*

Wherever I look
they tout six glorious figures

stations. mt. penance. the crash course. and
alien liturgy

Don't we

Better that I give
this to *you* to hold
because knowing me
I said (too trusting?)
but then I *had* to
come asking
didn't *I*
      A tree
comes down we get closer
we see too much of
each other don't
we I sound like
you and you get it from
me (obviously) the sky
grows more immense
the baby stops crying
the instant we leave the house
sometimes I aim for transparency
and even mention The Influence
in the Room (as if self-reflection
meant Redemption) I tell all
my selves and
sometimes the cupboard
gets loud and sounds like
the laundry or the
underground and well
we're watching this movie
aren't we and where there's History
there's this casual
moral parallel
telling us
It's a media trial but a Fiction
yes and we're all blameless here

Setting for a Theme

To live on the same street
as the school I can't attend
being always capable

in our best writing
uniforms

we do Belonging
pathology of a theme
now *concern now pre
occupation* now *Issue*

and the theme of the text wedded to it barely
registers
no matter how close we go?!

Merchant of Venice –
more anti-human
than anti-religious

Mending Wall's
narrator's serve on his
stone-age neighbour

the greater separation
the more loveless wall

preparation for
an exam called

The Trial

before a late afternoon
findaword to quell a miniriot

Friday pm.
pitch it low
real low

Blazers on platform 9
and like the other lolling heads
I sleep on the way home

and dream of a longer
commute

-

Like two sides to every single argument
Q&A's putting up
a few loons to solve its bias crisis
wedge the tables

Pride of New England's
tacky little lapel pins of nation
Pride o' the Shire's
        they're talking about

        religion
like The Merchant
of Venice
they never read

and one of these days
you're going to be able
to say whatever you
like to whoever you like

whenever you like

-

We go back

sharing a locker
and a secret

doing Be
Longing

(Two I remember in particular
though I still can't name them)

-

3:18: Theory's attentive restless bodies wait release no
        go back the chip packet
                no go back your

        chair

Recovery ode

Talk of the night before –

some moment of mirroring
 impasse in the corridor
  then nothing

what attenuates
the broken thread
 but news of a two-day
technical mishap

...dreaming
...guiltless
 but unsaved

on a liquid diet
        light duties

        Like all distant
droids insist their humanity

        some time

        you come in with

an open T showing only
 the letters "AMO"

        and I can't

 read and we're leaving

Now my minders say

(though *I'd* stay)

–

Here was my
Backwards glance

Beatty Hotel

When the pub closes

the publican

Dave

I think it's Dave

brings the bottle

of tequila

and an esky full of beer

and says

"would the last one to leave

mind turning off

the television."

A little trust

we agree and just

at last some relaxation

of the rules.

Camp park epic

To inflate this ample bed with your breath alone.

Communicating rooms

Behind a glass partition

wind stripping the last of an amber's colour. Blue

Days that expedite the end of cash the handwritten:

connecting us to feel that deficit between the digital

and tactile. I work in a kitchen. Marking double absences

and written speeches. Asking what happened to the

numbers in the non-compulsory.

-

In gallery the meeting room's on

five levels. Rooms in a block of flats. Lights out

if you're just a voice. Tuesday: deep in the mail…

We revise: Elective recluse…(before the internet)…

Privations…compensated…in some degree…by poetry.

Pets siblings and their bedroom cameos. Here we are –

plain-clothed in our other warmer lives.

-

Get up and walk around a bit for your back

and stretch. Just now you could hug Google

for a needle in a bookstack and plugs in an

argument. All the records I couldn't keep/

up with. My main issue in the office. Yet

time was more tensible here and work

entrusted to the home flatters me.

-

We're all at home

on a double island.

Exploding domestic

squares. That no interior

invert[*s*] *public space* no snowed-in dwelling

diminishes the entity of the outside world

only makes it.

-

Last summer as no memory

but what you see walking the street.

The picture books will talk us through it.

Sour patronage that necessitates Charity.

Flat reaction times. This morning

an aerial view of the city under heavy fog.

City towers. Islands.

-

Counting waves to austerity.

Jiggle the finance. Nominate

a status.

Married?

What? (Among the possessives I find

Girlfriend casual *Partner* business-y *De-*

facto cold. So I call you by your name.)

-

Not marriage

not even the internet or watching

our doubles on television

over decades prepared us.

We get outside for a change.

A more social face of commerce

communicating round a bank checkout.

-

Online dating is what it is.

The season's off.

The Arts are dead. Like cash

handwriting. What real change?

Spade-like leaves on a terrace.

A tree. A rosella then another.

In a tree. Its colour.

Conditions

Black type on a red and unforgiving ground

(wherein

meaning)

names in white on

a yellow —

strain on eyes widening to questions of

Visibility.

        Street light

        that flickered to life in the early

        growing dark that quit settings to

        conditions betraying how random

        the Program.

    Beneath

    which:

    Lichen

grows

on

trees.

                                      Dot of orange

                                      on the switch.

```
                 |     |     |     |     |     |     |
                 |     |     |     |     |     |     |
                 |     |     |     |     |     |     |
                 |     |     |     |     |     |     |
  _____     |     |     |     |     |     |     |
                 |     |     |     |     |     |     |
                 |     |     |     |     |     |     |
                 |     |     |     |     |     |     |
                 |     |     |     |     |     |     |
                 |     |     |     |     |     |     |
                 |     |     |     |     |     |     |
                 |     |     |     |     |     |     |
                 |     |     |     |     |     |     |
  X              \|/   \|/   \|/   \|/   \|/   \|/   \|/
```

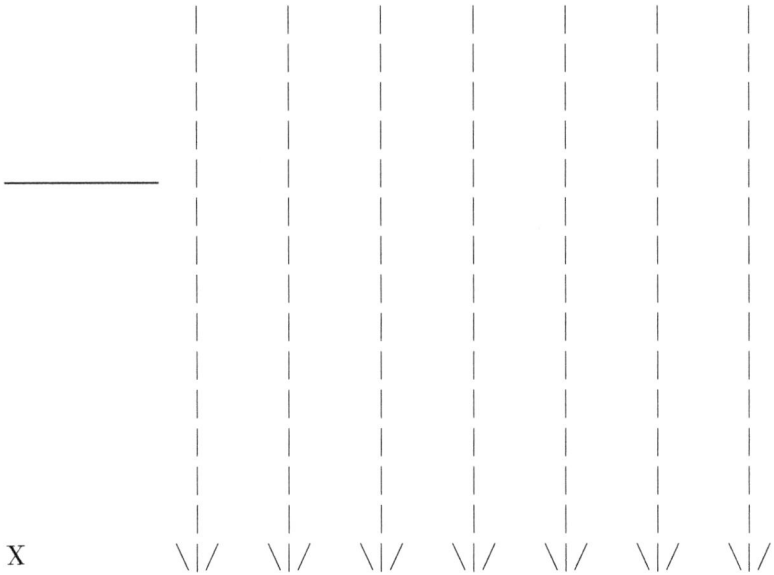

                                      Thus we navigate.

Dissimilar misty grey as lifts

the price of fuel

your rainbow

umbrella.

Sun. Too much.

Not

enough. After

months of locational trial and error

pale-bright flower.

Orange

West of Katoomba on every bit of your
brakes entring dubitable wine country.

Wellington Kirkconnell Lithgow Bathurst
prison country central New South Wales.

The view down to fortitude or optimism
crossing a bridge. Two motioned by tiny

no-tell internal dramas the whole way:
air pressure...How stress Canomodine?

New metalanguage rising off the palate.
Secret "hints" and "notes" though good.

Throw a blanket on three country pubs.
Favourite among the local toponymies —

Cadia...Mumbil...once gold-mining town
called Lucknow.

Untitled

The Dream itself to leave it all behind — so say the towers on the range.

    Soluble by Smiths or thereabouts
    at least the radio knows its limits.

It's lost now cue the audio romance. Windows green for miles. In a seam
less sympathetic build we'd live fairly *in* the hills make us snug between

    a pressed earth floor and moss roof
    and reconciled though secret nails

hold the place together. Coffee or conversation are what we need at this
midpoint. The road ramps off to playgrounds. Though all passengers are

    soundly entertained. Their ears cupped. It all
    streams by…cows the creek the trees the bell

birds…familiar song we could never put a face to. Again the radio
searching…coarse…but clearing: "What's on your mind Australia?"

    Annie Lennox: "must be talk-ing to an
    an-gel". (All attempts to sing along are
    doomed.) ....

Directions should be easier than this then I'm reading *Voss* on a verandahh.

    Where imagination eclipses history
    becomes history.

    No map as frontispiece but no notes.
    (No wonder then they get so lost.)

The book's a bargain hardback brick. Now closed. Bequeath it to the house.

Field

Planes on autumn blue
bums on blankets
breeze on a page
as if all it does is
court distraction
soft traffic sounds
memory of midnight amplified
in a working harbour
whimsy of
the street sign in woollens
warming the city
I guess
or was it art it was
outside the gallery

-

Its view to
Town or City
Hall...'s dual flags
as seem so much one
what maintenance
to put a life-like print
to the flaking surface
ex-posing the core
they made the platform
though not the view (the
sea) still we admired the
platform (for the view)

-

Every weekday

morning *Bushells*
slides by on the same
edifice huddled sheep
and clustered stone
higher up so that's
how you say Bowral
in the highlands an
arm spills from the
luggage rack looking
up from *The Lost Dog*
turning the colour
right up by Moss Vale
Country Club

-

American Canadians
censured by the self
appointed Australian
for a "way with words"
I almost say something
and here's your vantage
decision and alternative
any glimpse or landscape
like the internet can tell you
all poems are vast erasures
this all passes and oernight
your background
becomes a wide
desert dune

-

Txt (!) telling me
in Cape Leveque

you'll be out of reach
though here we're
wide round corners
rolling out *inter*prise
in the image of a bus
and what you deserve
is unrivalled (coverage)
so the world could be
constant to you
and be there always

-

Now the first whistle
classical figures in the field
now lest we flag in a deficit
of pure entertainment
shards of resistant rock
check the brief time
between stoppage and restart
spaces properties of
simple but unadorned
city spaces habitable
beyond intention
we come to you
you call down the code

read vacant sea

No apparent lines today
so no violent ellipses —

Where it's only water
quote 0 if not the body

Lit

and went on

in that place I never
meant to visit and

never left

Series ii

Body rolled

and rudely

        woken

late

        with unspeakable

        excuses

I plan

        picture

sound and

pad out the hour

        Mercy:

        my needles

twin-administered

        before

team meetings

best practice

                              meetings

a cold

                              plate and diction

                              not fit to repeat

in the home

                              We watch series

serially

                              thinking terms

                              of attention

of turning off

                              detached

from one strand

of a loosely

                              plaited

storyline

                              In this scene

                              a small disaster

on Broadway

cuts deeper

than Connor's

(Con's) failed

presidency bid

Mostly

absorbed

I laugh then

suddenly cease

to laugh

fearful now

of my instinct

Then I wake

then I dream

of old old friends

and wonder how such

distance and obscurity

attend our dreams...

Thursday:

The New World

        "Kiss and Ride"

is where we part —

        kiss? Keeping

        to ourselves

devices

        at the bus stop

Coffee to work

and other

        relationships

A moment's politesse

        as a cursory portal

        to core business

Briefly

        we live in worlds

without subtext:

who said anything

        about comparative

lives? And this

        sustains us

        Should I feel

ambivalent when you

        call an icon

of our study

"Some guy"

        raising the question

of idolatry

        "essence of enquiry"

        (we've covered

it) How slow

        today is progress

in its moment

of becoming.

                          Equity and signal

to all! we say

                          Work will not suffer

                          work will be less

possible without it.

                          We're in History:

we're watching

WWII in SD colour

                          we have it though

and this endless script

                          or vast store

                          of words and PICS (!)

that leaves

                          the future so much

less to infer

(of who we were)

If I overheard the distant capital correctly

It's another split shift and I buy time
by running my heart
up simulated hills and office blocks
while reading in the
glow of ten idle screens.
this walking path's more real
suitably popular and well-lit
though shrill nests fear me and over
sight rakes down the usual web.
so much that shouts out to be seen
that clingy moon all day at our side
graffiti up high and out of harm's way
oath proliferating on a lane
appealing discrepant
scripts like our story
overhearing yours
shops the lesser crimes
but more the dirt that any address
belies (or nosing enquete uncovers)
speaking on plath and domestic life as if
there were naturally anything to confess.
there's always a number to call
and surreal games that knock
at others' doors and ask *do* I *live here?*
lend unlikely counsel.
bright foam-capped lawns
crops of maize rocket peas
contest the bitumen verge
otherwise it's negri via nietzsche on
neighbourly love or *homo suburbiensus*
his thesis similitude and love's indicted
a kind of island private
if forever shared

where for all it's worth the vast horizon
backs a collective focal about-face.
piecing up their heart periapt
booty and buff in the infinity pool
under the hotel palms ready-to-settle
or next-sent-packing and jilted in paradise…
still i feel prone perhaps to a "surplus pathos".
our own june saw the may yield whittled
bare was saying about enough. while
conduit and cable test the castle walls
openness is always the better policy –
REAL "farthest" borderless
love taking in for instance
the member for dickson
truth and its non-neutrals
serving sweets dishing
terminal tags to later generations X, Y and…
handshakes that stand to futureproof us all.
gladly the weather brought relief.
frozen dinners were going cold tones
friendly as a doorbell politely imperative
when in scenes familiar enough the party
packed off to its own zones and devices.
who know our likes as well as any?
likes if not *dis*likes.
like an unbidden romp…pittance for
admission considering the catalogue
and what we receive.
kookaburras rang
earlier like perfect.
your niece is down from dubbo's bronx.
these streets seem safe
enough the blinds
not yet drawn on your giant television.
the music thumps

and fades as we pass.
then it's night enough
for singling out red antares
for blacking out most of massif
westfield and hungry jacks and JB and
the rest a local companion index.
tonight we have a stack of plans
but conversation seems enough.
time flies I stir the cup and
take out the bitterness.

Owing (+ adding) to saturation

Topical risk
(adds to saturation)

adds nothing

-

Trespass
        (just leaving
the house)

present landscape

        of a new domestic
        genre

Like even new reactive
England under Br/exit
got cold feet

        and forgot
to bolt

its doors
                in time

"There will be lots of death"

        We graph more
than finance like one

universal virus destroys another

yet the fear
that Present Landscape
vindicates an economic

model of leadership

If this is war
and if the Hilton's
"like a prison"

we've never been...

    (Blank

    comparison)

    So this

    "prison"

    (isolation)

Or...

all our little
ritual chancing on
essentially human

    discretionary law

We rehearse:

Just say…
just tell them

(you had
no wireless)

-

Why are we
alone here

why
not in prison

-

Amped late slotted
surf talk
on the stairs

Light
traffic passing

for the sound of the shore

Perplexed magnetism of the
particular Person of Interest
at the limit of an animated

leash

-

(Was all Yesterday
of retro
spective reliance)

-

Was all TV

-

How
many's
a crowd?

I dream more

-

The sea goes out grey to its limit

Today and tomorrow the only
place we've been

(Promise)

Big screen

Running the block in revised

style: min. impact

in motion

an elementary

animation

warming down

what appeals are

waves of mauve orange cloud

set like lava to the west

Beautiful. I don't use the word lightly

why don't I reduce it

to the small screen

in a waiting pocket

video and post it

-

Not *always* first from the office

you're off-duty

                    flat on the floor

in corpse or prone Christ pose

            more alive if

                trying not to reflect

gazing   up through closed venetians

            a tiled ridge   and satellite

        receiver   though no planes

                        fleet

        grounded

            -

            Two crimson in the callistemon

        endure the coincidence

suffer chance   and live with it

            pan to the incurious cat

            with the ♥ necklace

in the drive   "So cute"

            or *too* cute

            -

            the antenna

            the ancestral tree

and late glow backing

sponged black

            tips of eucalypts

            darker than night

            already

            the reserve

            -

This all happens on the big screen

like bats 1 hr early   flood the sky

(not quite)   but drowsy and erratic

feeling the way to where (?)

their night life

takes them

Blue Lounge

Swift escort for a placard un petit coup in how you pay.
Some goose eggs the whig in his ball cap and sobriquet.
And walks. Stealth-raked skies:
[O'] pyne's parting gift. How's
tricks in the harmy? As long
as your world stands still
washed out millennial fatigues are all context. If
you're leaving town the traffic's locked
and if you're staying.
There may be still be time.
Before the voiceover's right of attorney
pathetic fallacy apropos a voiceless environment.
So we communicate: design of open plan
living and what draws you in draws you out
(as if you weren't already in. In and of). Here
is my life in pictures and now my camera has
a phone. Though mostly we just txt.
High adventure in Belmont. In sub
urban Maitland or Charlestown City
the vision's renewal
the prize acquisitive
then why not keep it.
A few sunstruck cadets
though why in fickle History
is the audience
always standing be
hind the sovereign when he speaks.
Neon decorates
but mainly feeds off the wreck
and all of its regular treasures.
Among the medals and the lanyards
we go looking for a common ground.
Having lived our own rich histories

of oversight or underthinking where
dashing titles rhyme into self-parody.
(What could save them now?) We'd
like to think
for the trials of the past
we'd learn to speak again.
In the break we nick off
in the Escape —
for mountains the sound
of birds and frogs
and a failed media
moratorium. (Those digs:
you couldn't imagine
a less military dorm.)
Just lying there
rinsing the greens
dicing the carrots
clearing the mail
the FYIs
we cross sweet
Daisy Cousens —
vamp "Provocateur"
of the New Philosophy.
If they are doing their job
earning their keep
this reply (riposte?) is
hardly what they had in mind.
It is albeit from where we stand a test
case for how far the human voice will carry.
Sound travels this far. At least. The
metre spikes either way. Alone in
the studio. Widowed to my radio
in the midnight! Plain routine (to
night): my dream residency.

Lights of home

Woke up stockinged blindfolded disarranged over Ashgabat —
2 ½ romances surely about lands us at the crawling border —
Dulled unfaithful apples threatening the plague as you pay —
There were spectacular grounds for mistaking it for home —
Bold signs that read like mama and café like taxi and home —
Like all the pictures and promises the exotic couldn't keep —
The camirror in the cam-era fronting the same procession —
Except the pressures of capitalism were even greater here
And like the famed sun much in one's face and seemed to be
Cursing and then even stalking if soon ever after loving us —
For who in the single diminishing instant we had become —
Then the northern spring in bubble jackets our worlds —
Comparable commensurable separable teased apart in
Levels of address or an inimitable trick of the tongue
Frescoes of the eucharist or prayer lost language in the
Grammatical foundations and if we're nurtured in a tri
Angulated hearing on marbleveined stairs we bring that
piece of home with us that was waiting and cling to it

Till cup be hid

The mind:
so much as so little else on it –
Ere thrice my
glass mislaid!

-

Like in your eyes I
become the distant recent past.

-

Warm tenor.
Then Japanese.
Then Allegory:
where everything's about
onething else (what it's *really*
about).

-

Ahh the

very irresponsible
service of alcohol

and if this all takes me back

Involuntary Memory

changing
subject

\-

Chuffed moon.

(My glass!)

\-

And like Paul Weller
and Tory Crimes
played drums for The Clash.

\-

And the house on two clear levels
and the party out with invitations
(icy catalysts) that clearly define it

\-

50!

Decades travel poetry
still a "wilful
subjectivity"?

\-

In the open set
the desk's up for grabs

and not a song goes the distance
            even the dedicated

      my love
         and the dance

-

"getting late"

"still early"

Acknowledgements

Love and thanks to:

Juanita, Judy, Verenna and Krissy, Barb and Baz, Lyndall, Helen, Rob, and family;

Poets and friends in Newcastle, Sydney, and Melbourne for your generosity and support over the years;

Colleagues and students at WBHS;

The team at Puncher and Wattmann.

An earlier version of *hotel universo* was shortlisted for the Noel Rowe Poetry Prize. Many thanks to its judges and administrators.

Many thanks to The University of Newcastle and the Karen Thrift Poetry Prize, and to Karen's friends for their kind and loving support of poetry in Newcastle.

Poems in *hotel universo* have appeared in: *slender Volume* (chapbook), *A Slow Combusting Hymn* (anthology), *Overland, Southerly, Cordite, Pink Cover Zine, Mascara, Sappho Poetry Forum for Queers, Otoliths, The Age, Famous Reporter, Clambake, Rabbit.* Thank you to their staff, and editors: Tim Wright, Kit Kelen and Jean Kent, Toby Fitch, Keri Glastonbury, Kate Lilley, Liam Ferney, Lachlan Brown, Astrid Lorange, Corey Wakeling, Michelle Cahill, Suman Lahiry, Mark Young, Gig Ryan, Ralph Wessman, Claire Albrecht, Ella O'Keefe and Alan Wearne.

www.ingramcontent.com/pod-product-compliance
Lightning Source LLC
Chambersburg PA
CBHW030844090426
42737CB00009B/1104